Why I Love Roses

Roses are an addiction with me. I wait eagerly as those buds fatten in spring for my first sniff of their perfume, and I snip madly in summer to fill bowls with flowers that eventually shower their petals on the table.

Since I bought my first bush roses from a High Street store at the tender age of twelve, I've grown to love them more. They have an unequalled ability to survive in most situations, and modern breeders have imbued them with an even greater colour range and improved disease resistance.

Ask me which group of roses are my favourites and I would have to come down on the side of the shrubs - their flower form and scent especially appeals. But don't let anyone tell you that modern roses have lost that exquisite perfume. Demands made by gardeners have resulted in breeders not only producing finer flower shape, but in increasing their determination to capture those delightful fragrances as well.

In this book you will find the pick of the roses from the world's breeders. They are a hard bunch to please, and the roses they have chosen must maintain their reputation. All of them are readily available from nurseries and garden centres all over the country, and they represent superb value.

But then I'm hooked; and I don't just say that because roses are thorny! A garden without roses isn't a garden worth having.

Bush Roses

Bush roses are the popular garden roses you see everywhere. They all flower through summer and autumn.

By looking at the pictures and the symbols you can judge at a glance what they look like, how big they grow, and for which uses they are ideal. For a key to the symbols, see p72.

Many roses are named for a special reason, after people, places, special events and so on. Where there's a story worth telling behind the name, it's given in these pages.

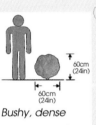

60cm (24in)
60cm (24in)

Bushy, dense

Abbeyfield Rose

ABBEYFIELD ROSE looks super when several plants are grouped together. It is named for Abbeyfield, the charity that provides homes for the elderly.

Amber Queen

In 1984 AMBER QUEEN was selected as Rose of the Year and has won many awards for its beauty, freedom of flower, and fragrance.

The blooms show up beautifully against its dark leaves.

No wonder it continues to be a top seller.

50cm
(20in)

60cm
(24in)

Cushiony, compact

Anisley Dickson

90cm
(36in)

←75→
(30in)

Upright, open

When this rose won the Royal
National Rose Society's major
prize, raiser Pat Dickson named it
for his wife. The large sprays are
so perfect that they often win
prizes at shows.

Anna Livia

Bushy, dense

ANNA LIVIA is the name given by James Joyce to the River Liffey in Dublin. The rose celebrates the City's millenium in 1988.

Baby Love

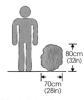

BABY LOVE is exceptionally healthy and among the most free flowering roses you can grow.

Upright, dense

Beautiful Britain

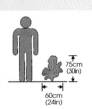

Bushy, uneven

The colour reminded the raiser of a variety of tomato, and he planned to call it MONEYMAKER. The Keep Britain Tidy Group suggested BEAUTIFUL BRITAIN instead. It was launched in 1983 as Rose of the Year.

Benita

Bushy, uneven

The frilly petal edges give BENITA's flowers special appeal. It's being grown in quantity as a "Breeders' Choice" selection.

Champagne Cocktail

100cm (40in)

70cm (28in)

Uprignt, open

This is a lively blend of ever-changing colours, always a talking-point for visitors. The name evokes the summer days in Ernest Dowson's poem:

They are not long, the days of wine and roses;
Out of a misty dream
Our path emerges for a while; then closes
Within a dream.

Christopher Columbus

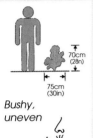

70cm
(28in)

75cm
(30in)

Bushy,
uneven

"Columbus sailed
the ocean blue in
fourteen hundred
and ninety two";
this striped novelty was named to mark the 500th
anniversary of his landfall - an extraordinary rose for
an extraordinary event.

Dawn Chorus

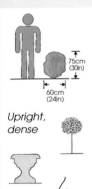

75cm
(30in)

60cm
(24in)

Upright,
dense

This neat grower makes a handy
perch for blue-tits in search of
greenfly once the "dawn chorus"
is over. Judges who voted it 1993
Rose of the Year were captivated
by the prettily furled buds.

City of London

Named for the City in 1988 to celebrate 800 years since it received its first charter from Richard I. The pretty scented flowers grow on long stems, and are excellent for buttonholes and arrangements .

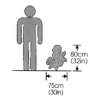

80cm (32in)

75cm (30in)

Bushy, uneven

75cm
(30in)

60cm
(24in)

Bushy, dense

Disco Dancer

DISCO DANCER seems an unlikely rose name - but when the scarlet flowers are lit by sunlight and waving in the breeze, the reasoning becomes clear. It's a wonderful rose for colour impact.

Elina

In Britain this was
introduced as
PEAUDOUCE, which
means "soft skin" in
French, and is a well
known brand of nappy.
Its alternative name
ELINA, already in use
abroad, is now preferred.
It's one of the very best
roses of recent years.

Upright,
open

Fellowship

FELLOWSHIP was named in Britain for the Rotary movement. In USA they call it LIVIN' EASY — not a bad name for a rose that flowers a lot and is trouble free.

Upright, dense

Freedom

Many consider FREEDOM the best yellow rose you can buy.

It always seems to be in flower.

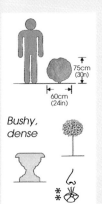

Bushy, dense

Flair

FLAIR is full of leaf and
flower, a splendid
choice for smaller
gardens where
maximum output is
essential, and a
"Breeders' Choice"
selection widely grown
for everyone to enjoy.

45cm
(18in)

45cm
(18in)

Cushiony,
compact

Fulton Mackay

75cm
(30in)

60cm
(24in)

Upright, open

The actor Fulton Mackay played the prison officer "Mr. MacKay" in the TV series Porridge. The rose named in his memory bears big flowers of graceful form.

Glad Tidings

A unnamed dark red rose was chosen as Rose of the Year for 1989. The question was - what to call it? Over lunch names were being tossed across the table. "Well, it's nearly Christmas" said nurseryman's wife Doris Tysterman, "so how about GLAD TIDINGS?"

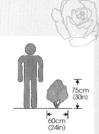

75cm
(30in)

60cm
(24in)

Upright, open

14

Golden Wedding

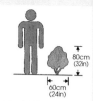

Upright, open

A GOLDEN WEDDING rose of 1938 became extinct. The raiser decided it was time to have another of that name, so useful as an anniversary gift.

Goldfinger

Bushy, uneven

This GOLDFINGER has nothing to do with James Bond. *Its sales benefit a charity, the Cancer and Leukaemia in Childhood Trust.*

Greenall's Glory

40cm (16in)

50cm (20in)

Cushiony, compact

It was a lucky day for the Manchester Parks foreman when he noticed, on a plant of REGENSBERG, a flower of different colouring. Thanks to his sharp eyes everyone can now enjoy it. The name derives from a firm of brewers, Greenall Whitley. "Days of beer and roses" may not sound at all right - but it's a splendid little rose.

Harvest Fayre

The name HARVEST FAYRE has an Olde English ring to it, but the rose comes from Ulster. It was voted Rose of the Year for 1990.

75cm (30in)

60cm (24in)

Bushy, uneven

Ice Cream

The cool name suits this big white confection of broad petals and rounded form. But nothing you find in a cornetto can match the delicate fragrance.

80cm (32in)

70cm (26in)

Upright, dense

Indian Summer

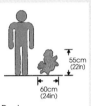

55cm
(22in)

60cm
(24in)

Bushy,
uneven

The muted apricot shades
of INDIAN SUMMER suggest
the gentle colours of an
autumn sunset.   And the
deep green leaves hint at
dark clouds behind - a
pleasing combination.
There's sweet fragrance
too.

Ingrid Bergman

The Swedish star must have been delighted with this splendid free flowering rose from the Danish raiser Poulsen. Red roses symbolise love. We are not told what Mrs. Poulsen had to say.

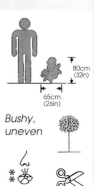

80cm
(32in)

65cm
(26in)

Bushy,
uneven

In the Pink

A neat grower with a good succession of shapely blooms.

90cm (36in)
60cm (24in)

Upright, open

Lovers' Meeting

The name comes from Twelfth Night.

75cm (30in)
75cm (30in)

Arching open

"...Trip no further,
pretty sweeting;
Journeys end in
lovers' meeting,
Every wise man's
son doth know."

20

Many Happy Returns

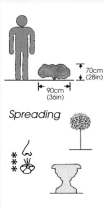

70cm (28in)

90cm (36in)

Spreading

Bred from an unusual line of parents, this grows like a low spreading shrub, covering itself in bloom. The name was suggested by, believe it or not - British Railways!

Melody Maker

70cm
(28in)

60cm
(24in)

Neat, upright

1991's Rose
of the Year
bears the
name of a
music
magazine.
The flowers
seem to
nestle among the dark leaves.

Michael Crawford

The star of stage and television is also President of a charity called The Sick Children's Trust, for which his rose was originally launched as a fund raiser.

80cm
(32in)

60cm
(24in)

Upright, open

Mountbatten

The very first Rose of the Year in 1982 honours Earl Mountbatten of Burma, under whom the raiser served in World War II.

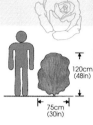

120cm (48in)

75cm (30in)

Upright, dense

***

Oranges and Lemons

An eye-catcher to surprise visiting friends.

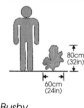

80cm (32in)

60cm (24in)

Bushy, uneven

**

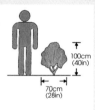

Upright,
open

100cm
(40in)

70cm
(28in)

Polar Star

POLAR STAR is a sturdy
bush from Germany
noted for the size of its
blooms.   It was launched
in Britain as Rose of the
Year 1985.

Paul Shirville

Mr. Paul Shirville was delighted to receive this fragrant beauty - an original idea for his retirement gift.

90cm (36in)
75cm (30in)

Bushy, dense

Remember Me

90cm (36in)
60cm (24in)

Neat, upright

Named for The Not Forgotten Association, which serves the interests of war veterans.

Remembrance

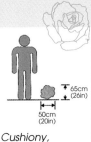

The Commonwealth War Graves Commission use this rose extensively in their plantings.

65cm (26in)

50cm (20in)

Cushiony, compact

Renaissance

What Alan Titchmarsh says about scent in modern roses certainly applies to this one. It is named for NADFAS.

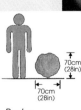

70cm (28in)

70cm (28in)

Bushy, dense

Rosemary Harkness

80cm (32in)

80cm (32in)

ROSEMARY HARKNESS has the sweetest of scents. The shape makes it ideal for buttonholes.

The raiser named it for his niece for her twenty-first birthday.

Bushy, dense

Royal William

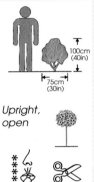

Upright, open

ROYAL WILLIAM was Rose of the Year jointly in 1987, and is one of the finest reds, giving long stems for cutting.

It was named for the 300th anniversary of the landing of William of Orange.

Savoy Hotel

The world famous
Savoy Hotel opened in
August 1889, and the
rose was launched for its
Centenary.   The colour
matches the napery
used there.

It's a strong grower
and remarkably
free blooming.

80cm
(32in)

60cm
(24in)

Bushy,
dense

Sexy Rexy

An oafish name for such a pretty rose? Don't be put off, it's lovely, and one of the best for a bed or group.

Upright, dense

Tango

Upright, dense

'Sexy Rexy' is the mother of TANGO, which shows how different roses can be even when closely related. The flamboyance of its brilliant blooms always makes people stop and look again.

Tequila Sunrise

This has many awards, thanks to its sturdy growth and the number of pretty flowers consistently produced.

Bushy, uneven

Toprose

This recalls not only the gardening brand name but also the Gold Medal won in its trials at Baden-Baden.

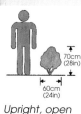

Upright, open

31

Valencia

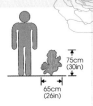

75cm
(30in)
65cm
(26in)

Bushy,

This scented
rose is popular
for the excellent
shape and clear
amber colour of
the large
blooms.

Vidal Sassoon

75cm
(30in)
60cm
(24in)

Bushy, uneven

The
lavender
brown
shades of
this
"Breeders'
Choice"
rose are
hard to
capture in
a picture but in the garden it attracts the eye.

Warm Wishes

110cm (42in)
70cm (28in)

The raiser considers WARM WISHES his best rose.

It has won major prizes for the quality of the large flowers and the freedom with which they are produced - and for fragrance too.

Upright, open

Patio Roses

Patio roses cater for areas where space is at a premium, and in a relatively short time these little beauties have become immensely popular. They can be planted in pots, tubs, window boxes, borders, beds; they make useful low hedges and are even at home mixed with alpines in the rock garden.

Their compact habit may vary from upright to spreading, with a height of generally no more than 60cm/24in. The most attractive ones have just the right balance between size and weight of stem, foliage and flower. No single factor should be out of proportion. 'Cider Cup', deep apricot, is an excellent example, having an upright habit, and carrying clusters of tiny blooms with high-pointed buds. Others, like 'Sweet Dream', 'Top Marks' and 'Ginger Nut' have cup shaped blooms, while those of 'Queen Mother' and 'Little Bo Peep' open flat. 'Sweet Magic' brings fragrance to the range.

Patio roses are hardy, enduring wind and frost, and they compare very well with bedding plants for colour, duration of flowering and value for money.

If small containers such as pots or window boxes are used, feeding will be necessary throughout the season, and sensible watering. Pruning should be done after the worst of the winter has passed. The majority of patio roses favour light pruning. Varieties with a more prostrate habit need to be cut back to retain their vigour every two or three years.

Patricia Dickson

Patio Roses

Cider Cup

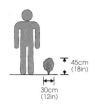

Neat, upright

A superb patio rose, like a scaled-down version of a bush rose.

Chatsworth

60cm (24in)

110cm (42in)

Spreading

CHATSWORTH, Rose of the Year for 1995, is bigger than most patio roses, and bears many flowers on arching stems.

Festival

FESTIVAL has unusual colours and was
introduced in 1994 as Rose of the Year.

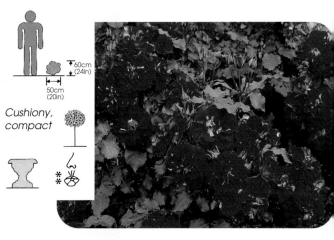

60cm
(24in)

50cm
(20in)

Cushiony,
compact

**

Fiesta

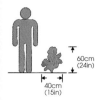

60cm
(24in)

40cm
(15in)

Bushy, uneven

*

FIESTA is a
1995 Breeders'
Choice with
pretty colour
patterns in its
petals.

Gentle Touch

The tiny urn shaped buds are perfect for small arrangements.

50cm (20in)

40cm (15in)

Neat, upright

Gingernut

GINGERNUT's name matches its "hot" colours.

40cm (15in)

45cm (18in)

Cushiony, compact

Little Bo Peep

*Don't miss LITTLE BO PEEP;
its petite cushionlike growth
smothered in dainty blooms is one of the prettiest
sights in the garden.*

30cm
(12in)

50cm
(20in)

*Cushiony,
compact*

---

*Shiny leaves
and rich
colouring make
this one of the
brightest patio
roses.*

*It was 1987 Rose
of the Year.*

Sweet Magic

35cm
(14in)

35cm
(14in)

*Cushiony,
compact*

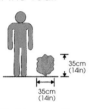

Pretty Polly

PRETTY POLLY gives a wealth of bloom on a neat rounded bush.

40cm (15in)

45cm (18in)

Cushiony, compact

** 🌼

Queen Mother

This pretty rose was named for the Queen Mother's 90th birthday.

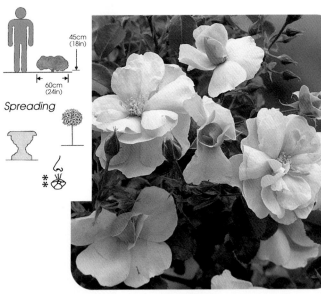

45cm (18in)

60cm (24in)

Spreading

Shine On

40cm (15in)

40cm (15in)

Cushiony, compact

This, in the raiser's words, "stands out in any crowd".

Sweet Dream

This very popular patio rose was Rose of the Year in 1988.

40cm (15in)

35cm (14in)

Neat, upright

Top Marks

TOP MARKS is linked to M&S and achieved "top marks" as 1992 Rose of the Year.

40cm (15in)

45cm (18in)

Cushiony, compact

Ground Cover Roses

Do you have an awkward area in your garden that has always been a nightmare to plant up? Maybe a steep bank, a neglected corner or even the top of a wall?

The versatility of the modern rose is such that many parts of the garden which were considered impractical for roses can now be readily planted up with ground coverers in the most unexpected situations. The type of plant required will provide colour for many months of the year, and will not be very demanding - a modest pocket of fertile soil cleared of perennial weed and a modicum of sunlight in the course of the day is all that is required.

Ground cover roses offer a wide choice of colour and growth.

The smallest grow six inches high and occupy some one and a half square feet. Others grow into immense spectacular rambling specimens six feet high and fifteen feet across, reminiscent of huge bramble bushes. In some varieties the autumnal harvest of hips provides extra unexpected colour.

All are simple plants to grow, requiring no pruning or other ritual maintenance. By definition they need to be disease resistant, but drenching them with a greenfly spray in spring is a wise precaution. Many are being propagated on their own roots, which eliminates the task of removing suckers. As with any other garden plants, for best results they need regular feeding. The modern ground cover rose has greatly contributed to the versatility of the world's favourite garden plant.

John Mattock.

Ground Cover Roses

Avon

Lowly AVON was a Breeders' Choice in 1993, and is excellent for a smaller space.

30cm (12in)

90cm (36in)

Creeping

*

Berkshire

60cm (24in)

100cm (40in)

Spreading

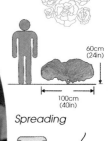

BERKSHIRE is an effective ground cover plant, bearing golden-eyed blooms on lax stems.

Blenheim

100cm
(40in)

140cm
(54in)

Spreading

BLENHEIM
combines
vigour, health
and freedom of
flower with old-style charm and fragrance.

Broadlands

BROADLANDS brings a new colour -
yellow - into ground cover roses.

75cm
(30in)

130cm
(54in)

Spreading

Flower Carpet

A healthy one to grow both as a standard (above) and as a ground cover rose (below).

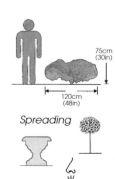

Spreading

Harewood

HAREWOOD is useful to plant in a group where moderate growth is needed.

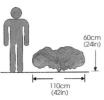

60cm
(24in)

110cm
(42in)

Spreading

Grouse

60cm
(24in)

300cm
(120in)

Creeping

With GROUSE you get sweet scent and extensive growth.

Kent

Bushes grow neat and rounded, with many short-stemmed blooms.

45cm
(18in)

90cm
(36in)

Spreading

Chilterns

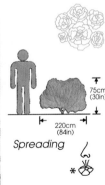

75cm
(30in)

220cm
(84in)

Spreading

This Breeder's Choice rose of 1994 is very suitable for larger spaces.

Pearl Meidiland

This gives useful cover near the front of a border.

70cm
(28in)

150cm
(60in)

Spreading

Red Meidiland

A variety that brings colour with both flowers and hips.

75cm
(30in)

150cm
(60in)

Spreading

Suma

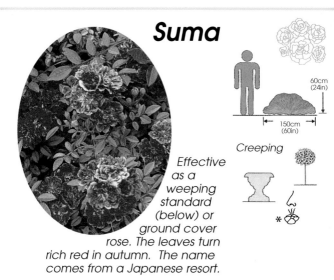

Effective as a weeping standard (below) or ground cover rose. The leaves turn rich red in autumn. The name comes from a Japanese resort.

60cm (24in)
150cm (60in)

Creeping

Surrey

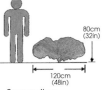

Spreading

The flowing habit of SURREY resembles a shallow pyramid sweeping to the ground.

Wiltshire

A Breeder's Choice for 1993, WILTSHIRE is compact.

Spreading

Hedge Roses

These are particularly useful to create a rosy barricade.

La Sevillana

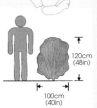

120cm
(48in)

100cm
(40in)

Upright,
dense

*

*LA SEVILLANA -
shrubby,
clothed with
foliage to the
ground*

The Seckford Rose

180cm
(60in)

100cm
(40in)

Upright,
dense

* *
* * *

*Upright, forms a
tough prickly
barrier*

Shrub Roses

Summer in England. Shrub roses tumbling all over the borders. I try to keep the colours sympathetic - no red with yellow - so that they can spend their days in harmony not arguing the toss. I love stripes on roses as I do on tulips - and of the ancient ones, 'Rosa Mundi' and 'Camaieux' are favourites. And I enjoy purples and lilacs. There's 'Tuscany Superb' which lolls about so - well, superbly; and 'Charles de Mills' which hangs over the path like some elderly roué after too much vintage port. Among the older roses, perhaps my favourite of all is 'Mme. Hardy', almost white but with that mysterious pale green centre...

But I'm neglecting the more recent shrub roses like 'Jacqueline du Pré'. What a beauty that is, and what a magnificent memorial to that intensely brilliant young cellist who died so tragically and so young. She played like one possessed as though her life depended on it and for a time, perhaps, it did.

I like 'Graham Thomas' and a rose called 'Heritage', and I've lighted upon 'Abraham Darby' which I don't have, and having seen its photograph, made a note that I should. One of its parents 'Aloha' is facing me as I write.

Roses are summer. We look forward to their blooming with huge excitement. Dread the final dead-heading, for it means another year gone. Perhaps that's one of the penalties of getting old, one becomes increasingly aware of mortality. Roses seem to epitomise the brevity of life and yet in that all-too-brief and glorious flowering they are truly magnificent. It's such an unfair standard for the rest of us to emulate.

Nigel Hawthorne

Francine Austin

90cm
(36in)

120cm
(48in)

Arching,
open

*Dainty sprays of the delightful FRANCINE AUSTIN
waving in the breeze create an airy, restful effect.
The raiser named this treasure for his daughter-in-law.*

Abraham Darby

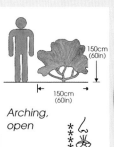

150cm (60in)

150cm (60in)

Arching, open

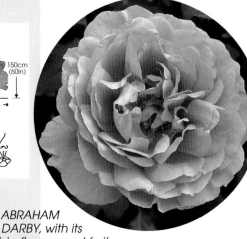

ABRAHAM DARBY, with its big flowers and fruity scent, is named after the builder of Britain's first iron bridge in 1777-79.

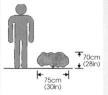

70cm (28in)

75cm (30in)

Spreading

Carefree Wonder

An excellent choice where a smaller shrub is wanted.

54

Bonica '82

BONICA '82 gives a wealth of flower through summer and autumn.

85cm (34in)

110cm (42in)

Spreading

120cm
(48in)

120cm
(48in)

Upright,
dense

Heritage

This is one of Nigel
Hawthorne's favourites.

The petals in the young
flower are infolded to give
the rose its prettily
'quartered' shape.

Graham Thomas

Rosarian and author Graham Stuart Thomas is honoured by this distinctive beauty.

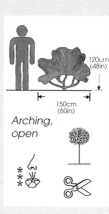

120cm (48in)

150cm (60in)

Arching, open

Gertrude Jekyll

150cm
(60in)

90cm
(36in)

Arching,
open

This scented rose is named
for the lady who greatly
influenced garden design,
teaching that gardens
should be places of natural
beauty.

Jacqueline du Pré

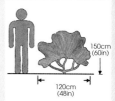

Jacqueline du Pré chose this sweet scented rose to bear her name.

It flowers unusually early, and continues through summer and autumn.

Arching, open

Climbers are special

I love roses, especially climbing roses. When I see pictures of thatched Victorian cottages with 'Mme. Alfred Carrière' climbing round the door, or remember the heady fragrance of 'Zéphirine Drouhin' growing up the walls of a sunny terrace, my heart melts and I feel happy just thinking of the wonders of England on a summer's afternoon.

Climbing roses have been a life saver in my small walled London garden, breaking the view between the garden and the flats beyond. From late May for the next few months the pale pink 'New Dawn' and the strong pink 'Aloha' grow through the jasmine and honeysuckle, and make me smile every time I look out of the kitchen window. This year I intend to plant another pink, 'Compassion' for its heavenly fragrance, and a new one called 'City Girl', which I look forward to enjoying in the summers to come.

The lovely thing about climbers is that they are so versatile, and with imagination, can be used in many ways to great effect. The new 'Nice Day' is one of the new miniature climbers, which are good for disguising unsightly corners, and the sweet smelling pink 'High Hopes' will grow vigorously to vary the height in a border. Climbing roses are great for fences and walls, for creating an arbour, clambering on a tree, or for making a run-of-the-mill cottage look picturesque.

One thing I find with climbers is that it is important to be patient. They need time to get established and have to be nudged into shape slowly, but once they get going, there's no stopping them. I love them.

Susan Hampshire

Breath of Life

The name of this pretty apricot to pink rose was suggested by The Royal College of Midwives to celebrate its centenary in 1981.

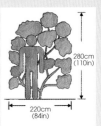

280cm (110in)

220cm (84in)

Climbing

High Hopes

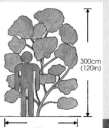

300cm
(120in)

220cm
(84in)

Climbing

HIGH HOPES is
vigorous and a
good one if you
want quick results.

Crimson Cascade

Like all the climbers in this book, CRIMSON CASCADE makes a brave show from summer through to autumn.

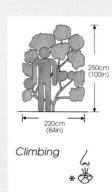

250cm
(100in)

220cm
(84in)

Climbing

Leaping Salmon

The big flowers of LEAPING SALMON have lovely form.

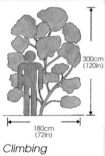

300cm
(120in)

180cm
(72in)

Climbing

The next section illustrates a recently developed group of roses, the miniature climbers.

These are very useful for maximum flower impact in limited space.

Miniature Climbers

Laura Ford

LAURA FORD honours the memory of a beloved wife and mother.

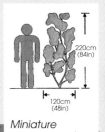

220cm (84in)

120cm (48in)

Miniature climber

***

Climbing Orange Sunblaze

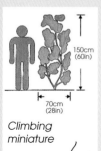

150cm
(60in)

70cm
(28in)

Climbing
miniature

*This brilliantly coloured
variety is a good choice
where space is limited.*

Nice Day

Now every gardener can literally "have a NICE DAY", not only in the garden but indoors as well, for the neat flowers of this Breeders' Choice rose are excellent for petite arrangements.

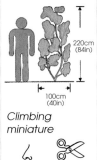

220cm
(84in)

100cm
(40in)

*Climbing
miniature*

Good as Gold

Climbing miniature

200cm (75in)
150cm (60in)

This catches the eye with its big sprays, and always seems to be in flower.

Warm Welcome

WARM WELCOME is always busy putting out new flowers.

Climbing miniature

220cm (84in)
220cm (84in)

A Rose By Any Other Name...

The names for the roses in the book are as used in the UK. Sometimes they are offered under a different name elsewhere. For example, 'Savoy Hotel' is sold as 'Integrity' in New Zealand.
To prevent confusion each variety has a registered name to identify it, whatever selling name is used. The registered names for the roses are:

Abbeyfield Rose - Cocbrose; Abraham Darby - Auscot; Amber Queen - Harroony; Anisley Dickson - Dickimino; Anna Livia - Kormetter; Avon - Poulmulti; Baby Love - Scrivluv; Beautiful Britain - Dicfire; Benita - Dicquarrel; Berkshire -Korpinka; Blenheim - Tanmurse; Bonica '82 - Meidomonac; Breath of Life - Harquanne; Broadlands - Tanmirsch; Carefree Wonder - Meipitac; Champagne Cocktail - Horflash; Chatsworth - Tanotax; Chilterns - Kortemma; Christopher Columbus - Poulstripe; Cider Cup - Dicladida; City of London - Harukfore; Crimson Cascade - Fryclimbdown; Dawn Chorus - Dicquasar; Disco Dancer - Dicdance; Elina - Dicjana; Fellowship - Harwelcome; Festival - Kordialo; Fiesta - Macfirinlin; Flair - Dicrelax; Flower Carpet - Noatraum; Francine Austin - Ausram; Freedom -Dicjem; Fulton Mackay - Cocdana; Gentle Touch - Diclulu; Gertrude Jekyll - Ausbord; Gingernut - Coccrazy; Glad Tidings - Tantide; Golden Wedding - Arokris; Goldfinger - Pearoyal; Good as Gold - Chewsunbeam; Graham Thomas - Ausmas; Greenall's Glory - Kirmac; Grouse - Korimro; Harewood - Taninaso; Harvest Fayre - Dicnorth; Heritage - Ausblush; High Hopes - Haryup; Ice Cream - Korzuri; Indian Summer - Peaperfume; Ingrid Bergman - Poulman; In The Pink - Peaverity; Jacqueline du Pré - Harwanna; Kent - Poulcov; La Sevillana - Meigekanu; Laura Ford - Chewarvel; Leaping Salmon - Peamight; Little Bo Peep - Poullen; Many Happy Returns - Harwanted; Melody Maker - Dicqueen; Michael Crawford - Poulvue; Mountbatten - Harmantelle; Nice Day - Chewsea; Oranges and Lemons - Macoranlem; Orange Sunblaze Climbing - Meijikatarsar; Paul Shirville - Harqueterwife; Pearl Meidiland - Meiplatin; Polar Star - Tanlarpost; Pretty Polly - Meitonje; Queen Mother - Korquemu; Red Meidiland - Meineble; Remember Me - Cocdestin; Remembrance - Harxampton; Renaissance - Harzart; Rosemary Harkness - Harrowbond; Royal William - Korzaun; Savoy Hotel - Harvintage; Sexy Rexy - Macrexy; Shine On - Dictalent; Suma - Harsuma; Surrey - Korlanum; Sweet Dream - Fryminicot; Sweet Magic - Dicmagic; Tango - Macfirwal; Tequila Sunrise - Dicobey; The Seckford Rose - Korpinrob; Top Marks - Fryministar; Toprose - Cocgold; Valencia - Koreklia; Vidal Sassoon - Macjuliat; Warm Welcome - Chewizz; Warm Wishes - Fryxotic; Wiltshire - Kormuse.

All these roses are offered in the UK through The British Association Representing Breeders (BARB), 9 Portland Street, King's Lynn, PE30 1PB

BARB

Get the best out of your roses

Roses are easy to grow; these are some basic guidelines.

A GOOD SITE

- an open sunny position, away from trees or large shrubs.

SUITABLE SOIL

- well drained, reasonably fertile. It's important not to plant new roses in ground where existing rose plants have long been established. Either replace with soil from part of the garden where roses have not been growing, or choose a fresh site, or us a a soil steriliser such as Armillatox.

THE RIGHT PLANTS

- buy quality roses from nurserymen or garden centres you can rely on; ask advice if in doubt what to have.

PREPARING THE SOIL

- dig the ground to clear it of weeds, mix in old manure, compost, leafmould or other available food; do this a month before you intend to plant.

PLANT CORRECTLY

- firmly and at the right depth - as shown.

PRUNING

- basic advice is to cut bushes and patios the first spring after planting to leave only 3-4in on each stem; and give other types a light trim. Visit one of the pruning demonstrations given in spring by the Royal National Rose Society and by nurseries and garden centres.

AFTER CARE

- for new plants, check they have stayed firm, tread round them and water any that are slow to produce leaves in spring; apply rose fertiliser when they begin to grow. - for older plants, mulch them (i.e. cover the soil between them) to feed them and improve the soil; garden centres stock many suitable materials. Use rose fertiliser when they begin to grow. Spray if you need to but remember that good plants properly grown and fed will better resist nature's troubles.

Learn to enjoy your roses more with

THE ROYAL NATIONAL ROSE SOCIETY
Chiswell Green, St Albans,
Herts. AL2 3NR
(Tel 01727-850461)

PETER HARKNESS on ...

Roses of the Future

In this book we see roses of many different shapes and colours - and every one of them has been introduced within the last fifteen years.

That shows how fast the rose family is evolving. And this process continues as breeders in many lands strive to raise new and better forms - better in health, strength, fragrance, beauty and freedom of flower.

For the future, who knows what we may expect? Roses that are thornless - or evergreen - or blue - with fragrant foliage - new colour patterns - bearing flowers in spikes and spirals - repellent to aphids - resistant to disease? All these aims are being pursued, as breeders work to bring them to perfection.

Already the rose is the most versatile family of garden plants. There's no lack of excitement as we contemplate what its future holds.

Key to the Symbols

 Small flowers

 Medium flowers

 Large flowers

 Especially suitable for growing in containers

 Available as a Standard

 Especially useful to cut and arrange

Fragrance Rating

Strong
Good
Moderate
Light

The plant sizes shown are what may be expected in normal UK growing conditions. The fragrance ratings are based on the editor's nose, and he is in full agreement with its findings.

Roses described as "Rose of the Year" or "Breeders' Choice" have been selected by growers and breeders as varieties that are easy to grow and most likely to give pleasure to gardeners.